# LIFE FILES

# SEX MATTERS

### JULIAN COHEN

Evans

# EVANS BROTHERS LIMITED

Published by Evans Brothers Limited
2A Portman Mansions
Chiltern Street
London W1M 1LE

British Library Cataloguing in Publication Data.
A catalogue record for this book is available
from the British Library.

First published 1997

Printed in Hong Kong by Dah Hua
Printing Co. Ltd.

ISBN 0 237 51653 5 (paperback)

# ACKNOWLEDGEMENTS

**Editorial:** Su Swallow
**Design:** Neil Sayer
**Production:** Jenny Mulvanny

**Cover** Jennie Woodcock/Reflections
**page 7** Marc Grimberg/Image Bank **page 9**
Edward Parker/Hutchison Library **page 10** Rex
Features **page 11** Rex Features **page 12** Steve
Niedorf/Image Bank **page 14** Jennie
Woodcock/Reflections **page 16** Thomas
Haley/Rex Features **page 17** Rogan Coles/Link
**page 19** Martin Dohrn/ Science Photo Library
**page 20** The Sun/ Rex Features **page 23** (left)
Hattie Young/Science Photo Library (right)
Eamonn McNulty/Science Photo Library **page 25**
Paul Brown/Rex Reatures **page 27** Barry
Lewis/Network **page 28** Ivan Coleman/Link
**page 30** Rex Features **page 31** John
Greim/Science Photo Library **page 34** Sally and
Richard Greenhill **page 35** Orde Eliason/Link
**page 37** Hattie Young/Science Photo Library
**page 38** David Weintraub/Science Photo Library
**page 39** John Greim/Science Photo Library
**page 41** Amanda Knapp/Rex Features **page 43**
Orde Eliason/Link **page 44** Custom Medical
Stock Photo/Science Photo Library **page 45** Ken
Cedeno/Rex Features **page 47** Rose
Marston/Rex Features **page 49** Jennie
Woodcock/Reflections **page 51** News Team
International **page 52** Jennie
Woodcock/Reflections **page 55** Rick Colls/Rex
Features **page 56** Barry Lewis/Network

# CONTENTS

# INTRODUCTION

> **Sex is the human activity which above all others generates vast amounts of vehemently-held opinion founded upon little (if any) basis of facts. It is the prime stamping-ground of the tribe of glib moralisers whose minds are firmly made up, in the teeth of whatever evidence there is.**
>
> Antony Grey *Speaking of Sex* Cassell 1993

In this book I examine some of the main issues concerning sex and sex education for young people. I have been strongly influenced by my experience as a teacher, youth worker and father and as a writer of sex education materials. I believe that young people today need to be 'sexually aware' so they can make their own, informed decisions about sex. At a time when we are trying to live with the consequences of HIV and AIDS this is more important than ever. Too often young people are denied what I believe should be their right - accurate information about sex and the many complex issues involved.

The book has been written within a definite moral framework. My moral framework is not one that tells young people what they should believe or do in their sex life (as long as it does not knowingly damage other people). Your choices in your sex life and views may be different from mine and that is your right.

The moral framework I have written within includes:
- Respecting ourselves
- Accepting responsibility for our own sexual behaviour
- Respect for, and tolerance towards, other people who may have different views than our own or different sexuality
- The right to information, education and helping services.

Sex education should be about open discussion of what are often very complex issues.

I would welcome your views about this book. You can write to me at
Evans Brothers
2A Portman Mansions
Chiltern Street
London W1M 1LE

Julian Cohen

> **As a species we're fascinated, compelled, confused, scared and in awe of sex.**
>
> Nick Fisher *Your Pocket Guide to Sex* Penguin 1994

# WHAT DO WE MEAN BY SEX?

Strictly speaking, the word 'sex' refers to the gender of people - whether they are male or female. However, the word sex has come to have many different meanings and how people think of sex today is often very different from the past.

One way to appreciate all the different ways we now think of 'sex' is to list some of the words that are commonly associated with it. The word 'sex' is often followed by the words:

appeal, attack, change, discrimination, drive, education, equality, life, object, problems, role, starved, survey, symbol, talk, therapy.

'Sex' may be preceded by such words as:

anal, conventional, explicit, first, oral, penetrative, pre-marital, safer and under age.

'Sexual' and 'sexually' are also followed by many words including:

abuse, active, aggression, aware, behaviour, career, chemistry, exploitation, fantasy, freedom, habits, harassment, intercourse, liberation, maturity, orientation, performance, revolution, risks, satisfaction, transmitted diseases, and values.

**Question**
What other words do you associate with sex? Does it matter what words you use to discuss sexual matters?

Sex can mean very different things to different people.

You can see that the word sex can have many different meanings, depending on the other words with which it may be linked.

## WHAT IS SEXUALITY?

Sexuality refers to people's feelings about being male or female and how they deal with these feelings. People may explore their sexuality by themselves through sexual feelings, touching themselves, fantasy or masturbation. They may also explore their sexuality through contact with other people. Heterosexuality refers to sexual feelings and relationships between males and females. Homosexuality refers to sexual feelings and relationships between people of the same

sex. Homosexual men are usually known as gay men. Homosexual women are usually referred to as lesbians. Bisexuality refers to people who are attracted to, and may have sexual relationships with, both men and women. Celibacy is when someone chooses not to have sexual relationships. Our sexual preference is not necessarily fixed and may change over our lifetime.

## DIFFERENT VIEWS OF SEX

For some people the main, and sometimes only, purpose of sex is to have children. This view usually suggests that sex should only involve heterosexuals having vaginal intercourse within marriage and that other forms of sex are unnatural or immoral. Use of contraception may be opposed as it prevents or reduces the possibility of a woman becoming pregnant.

Sex can also be seen as physical activity. This way of thinking about sex focuses on what people actually do, both to themselves and with each other. Many people think of sex in this way as only being about intercourse. When the term 'sexually active' is used people

> 66 One of the most striking changes in recent times has been the acceptance of sex as a valid expression of intimacy and a source of pleasure divorced from procreation. Another major change is that sex is now out in the open. Probably never before has sex been so openly displayed and publicly discussed as it is today. 99
>
> The Diagram Group *Sex: A User's Manual* New English Library 1981

### Question
What differences may there be in the way men and women view sex? Why do these differences exist?

### Find out!
Find out about how people have viewed sex in the past and how different religions or cultures see sex.

Some people think that sex should only take place within marriage but for most people in the UK, sex begins before marriage.

> **We are preoccupied by sex. Sex has become...a commercial product - the promised prowess of the car ads, the self-seeking singing of Madonna. It has turned into a marker of adult identity, so if you don't do it you're not a proper adult....But what exactly has sex become on the level of 'ordinary' people's real lives?**
>
> Ann Oakley *The Independent on Sunday* 23rd January 1994

usually mean intercourse, even though there are many other ways people can be sexually active, such as masturbation, oral sex, fantasy or even stroking and kissing.

For many people one of the main purposes of sex is to express intimacy, commitment and caring to one's partner. In other words sex can be about an expression of love between people and is often seen as an important part of a long-term relationship.

Sex can be seen as being about pleasure - about having positive physical and emotional feelings about oneself and towards others. It is only in recent years, with the development of more effective contraceptives such as the pill, that sex has been separated from having children and been seen in this way.

However, for some people sex - particularly sex outside marriage - is viewed as a sin. Sexual emotions and experiences may be seen as shameful and result in feelings of guilt. This view of sex is often associated with strong religious views.

Sex is also associated in some people's minds with

## Question

**'Sex should only take place within long-term, loving relationships.' What do you think?**

disease and illness. In the past people, especially women, who openly enjoyed sex were seen as being mentally ill and in need of treatment. Today, some people still believe that homosexuals, or other people that do not fit their own sexuality, have a disease.

Sex can also be about power and money. Examples include prostitution, pornography and the use of sex to advertise and sell products. Some people also say sex is a

commodity that is exchanged for money in many relationships and that this is common in traditional heterosexual marriages where the man works and the woman is a housewife with no independent income.

Sex can also sometimes be about abuse and violence. This includes rape, child abuse, sexual harassment and all sexual interactions where one person has not fully consented. Most, but not all, sexual abuse and violence is committed by men on women.

## Find out!

Survey how the media view sex. You might watch television programmes and adverts, look at newspapers and magazines, review films or videos.

Sex Is used to sell many everyday products.

# WHAT ARE THE TRENDS IN YOUNG PEOPLE'S SEXUAL BEHAVIOUR?

## THE RECENT PAST

Sexual behaviour and attitudes towards sex have changed dramatically in Britain and many other developed countries in the last 30 years. Until the late 1960s sex was not openly discussed and effective contraception was not widely available. Sex was regarded by many as something that only took place within marriage for the purpose of having children. Divorce was relatively rare and restricted by law. Male homosexuality was illegal until 1967 and abortion was very restricted until 1968.

The idea that people could and should enjoy sex in itself was not common, particularly for women. The

Marriage is as popular today as ever but in the past divorce was much less common.

introduction of the contraceptive pill in the 1960s meant that the link between intercourse and having children was broken. This, together with the desire for more personal freedom, has led to many changes in sexual behaviour.

## CHANGES IN MARRIAGE AND FAMILIES

In Britain today people are marrying and having children at a later age and having fewer children. Whilst marriage is almost as popular today as ever, divorce rates have increased significantly. In the early 1900s less than one per cent of marriages ended in divorce. By the early 1970s it was 10 per cent and rising. Now about one in three marriages in Britain end in divorce.

There has also been an increase in the number of women who have children outside marriage. About 30 per cent of children are born outside marriage. More women either live with children by themselves or co-habit, rather than marry. By 1991 nearly one in five families with dependent children were single-parent families, the highest figure for all European countries. In Britain today less than 30 per cent of families with children involve a male breadwinner, housewife and two children in a first marriage. The living situation of most adults and children is no longer the stereotypical 'nuclear family'.

This is how we often think of a family but today families come in many shapes and forms.

# A NATIONAL SURVEY

A recent survey of sexual attitudes and lifestyles in Britain interviewed nearly 19,000 people aged 16 to 59. It is the largest survey of its kind ever carried out in this country. The aim of the survey was to find out how health education campaigns to combat HIV and AIDS could be more effective.

The British National Survey found that of people born in the 1930s and 1940s (now aged 55 to 65 years) 38 per cent said they were virgins when they married. Of those born in the late 1960s and early 1970s (now in their twenties) less than one per cent were virgins when they married. The researchers concluded that first sex within marriage is now very rare.

Young people today are also likely to have had more sexual partners than older people. Whilst a small minority have many sexual partners, the majority practise what is called 'serial monogamy' - they stop having sex with one person before they start another sexual relationship, rather than have lots of partners at the same time.

# FIRST SEXUAL EXPERIENCE

One key finding of this survey is that young people today have their first experiences of sexual intercourse at a younger age. The average age of first intercourse for the 55 to 59-year-olds in the British National Survey was 21. For the 16 to 24-year-olds interviewed, the average age of first intercourse was 17. About one third of 16-year-olds have experienced intercourse. The survey also found that initiation into sexual activities such as kissing, cuddling and petting was also happening at a much earlier age today. Sexual activity (as opposed to sexual intercourse) is common today across the secondary school age range.

# MATURING EARLIER

In the 1860s the average age at which girls reached puberty and had their first period was 16 to 17 years old. The age of puberty has continually fallen over the last 100 years. By the early 1960s the average age for a girl to have her first period was 13 and a half and many people believe it is now even younger. In 1860 boys reached full growth at around 23 years old. By the early 1960s this had fallen to 17 years old. In other words young people are maturing physically and sexually at an earlier age.

# TEENAGE PREGNANCY

In recent years there has also been an increase in the number of teenage girls in Britain who become pregnant. More than 8,000 under-16 girls become pregnant in Britain each year although this has recently

## Question
'Young people today are too quick to get involved in sexual relationships'. What do you think?

Teenagers today are physically mature at a younger age. For this and other reasons young people's sexual behaviour is very different from 100, even 30 years ago.

fallen slightly. However, the proportion of young girls who are having intercourse and become pregnant has actually fallen. In other words, although many, and clearly too many, teenage girls and boys fail to take adequate precautions against pregnancy, a higher proportion do than was the case in the past. Young people today are more likely to use contraceptives when they have intercourse than their parents' generation, even though surveys show that for over half of under-16 girls, contraception is not used when they first have intercourse.

Britain has the highest teenage pregnancy rate in Europe (America has the highest rate of all developed countries) and over half these pregnancies end in abortion. Young people in Britain are not, on average, having intercourse at a younger age than in other European countries but they are less likely to

use contraceptives. Boys as well as girls need to ensure they use contraceptives properly if they have intercourse.

## OTHER SEXUAL PRACTICES

The British National Survey also found that young people today are more likely to have experienced a range of sexual behaviours other than vaginal intercourse, such as oral sex and mutual masturbation. They are more interested in satisfying their partners sexually and exploring different ways of being sexual. A number of studies have also suggested that young people today, and especially girls, may masturbate more than in the past.

> **Masturbation is, for most people, the introduction to their sexuality...In the last century, children were told that masturbation causes blindness, tuberculosis and a softening of the bones.** "

Kate Saunders and Peter Stanford *Catholics and Sex* Heinemann1992

It is clear that sex is no longer seen as something that only men derive pleasure from. A number of surveys have shown an upward trend in the reported rate of female orgasm. Women are now seen as being more equal sexual partners who have their own sexual desires and needs.

This may have something to do with more liberal attitudes to sex and the feeling that sex should - at least in part - be about pleasure. It may also have something to do with the threat of HIV and the message that safer sex involves practices other than intercourse (see chapter 3).

## Question
**In what different ways have changes in young people's sexual behaviour affected men and women?**

Surveys suggest that the number of gay men and lesbian women has probably not changed much although the fact that there is now more openness about homosexuality means people are more willing to talk about it. The British National Survey of people of all ages reported that just over six per cent of men and three per cent of women reported having had a homosexual experience although some surveys have given higher numbers. The figures were very different in different areas of the country. Twelve per cent of men interviewed in London said they had experienced a homosexual relationship. This may indicate that gay men may choose to live in parts of the country where there are more social and health facilities for them.

## PROSTITUTION AMONG YOUNG PEOPLE

Prostitution has been with us for thousands of years. Today this includes young female, and some young male prostitutes. It is not clear whether prostitution has actually increased in recent years or whether it is just being talked about more openly. However, some people believe that, during the 1980s and 1990s, the increase in homelessness and unemployment amongst the young, together with cuts in welfare benefits, has led to more young people being involved in prostitution. Child prostitution is far more common in poor developing countries, where some young people are forced to cater specifically for wealthy businessmen from developed countries. There have been recent attempts to introduce new laws to prosecute British men who have sex with child prostitutes in other countries.

> **Improvements in contraceptive technology, earlier puberty, the rise of feminism and much greater mobility have all contributed to a changed atmosphere... with sex (as with drugs), public debate has trailed reality.**
>
> *The Independent* November 1995

# CONCLUSION

Patterns of sexual behaviour amongst young people have changed dramatically in the UK in the past 30 years. Similar trends have been found in other developed countries, although different countries have different patterns influenced by religion, law and culture.

Most people have a sexual career. It changes over time. Some people are only involved in heterosexual relationships throughout their life. Some only have homosexual relationships. Some people are attracted towards or have relationships with both men and women over their lifetime. Still others remain celibate and are not involved in any sexual relationships. At one stage people may have one stable relationship. At other times they may have a number of different partners. Sometimes sex is very pleasurable and frequent. At other times it may be unpleasant or infrequent. There is no one 'normal' pattern of sexual career. It varies for each individual.

How we feel and what we do when we are young may have little bearing on what happens to us in future. It helps to remember this. We need to avoid having unrealistic expectations of ourselves and other people and accept the variety of human sexual needs and experience.

## Question
**Do you think the trends in young people's sexual behaviour are a good or bad thing?**

Two young women who are glad to be gay.

# WHAT ARE THE RISKS OF HAVING SEX?

Sex can be a very pleasurable experience. Sex can be about sharing and caring. It can be fun. But sex can also be risky, especially if you are young. In what ways can sex be risky and what can young people do to minimise the risks?

## EMOTIONAL RISK

There is a lot of pressure to have sex - whether it involves intercourse or not. One risk is that people will get involved in sex when they are not really ready. It might be that they are too young and immature. It might also be that they are not ready for sex with a particular person or in the situation in which

> **In a recent large survey of adults in the UK over one in four women and one in eight men said they thought they had intercourse too early.**

Some situations can lead to sexual involvements which are later regretted.

they find themselves. They may later regret their decision to have sex or to be involved in certain sexual activities and feel bad about it afterwards.

In 'Mizz' magazine a survey of teenage girl readers in 1994 found that nearly one third had felt pressurised to have sex before they were ready. The main pressure came from boyfriends but some came from other girls. Boys also feel pressures to have sex when they are not sure they want to, but they may be less likely to openly admit it.

Another important factor in the survey was alcohol. A number of girls said they had sex (sometimes without using contraception) after getting drunk and getting 'carried away'. Other surveys have shown that taking drugs like cannabis and ecstasy has contributed to young people having sex when they are not sure about what they are doing.

---

### Some bad reasons for having sex:

'All my friends are doing it.'
'I will hurt his/her feelings if I don't.'
'I've got to do it sometime.'
'He/She will dump me if I don't.'
'Friends will laugh at me if I don't.'
'He/She will think I'm frigid.'
'It will make him/her love me.'
'He/She will go out with me if I do.'
'He/She will find someone else if I don't.'
'Lots of people will fancy me if I do.'
'He/She paid for me to go out.'
Threats such as 'If you don't I will...'
'I'll look stupid if I don't.'
'It will give me a baby.'
'It will show I'm grown up.'
Emotional blackmail: 'Don't you love me then?'
'I want to be accepted.'

---

> **66 Drug and alcohol use can lower inhibitions and make it more difficult to avoid unwanted sex or use contraceptives effectively. 99**

Having sex when you are not sure you want to can leave you feeling bad afterwards. You may feel disappointed that it did not live up to expectations. You may think you failed to excite your partner and feel a failure. You might feel guilty and awkward. You may worry that whoever you were with will tell other people. You may worry that your parents will find out. It may leave you feeling quite lonely and confused.

## RISK OF PREGNANCY

If a boy and a girl have vaginal intercourse there is obviously a risk that the girl could become pregnant. Britain has a very high teenage pregnancy rate compared to most other European countries.

Far fewer teenage girls become pregnant in countries such as the Netherlands, even

> **66 In Britain, more than 100,000 teenage girls become pregnant each year and about 8,000 are under 16. 99**

---

### Question

'Fifteen years old is too young to have sexual intercourse.' What do you think?

---

A pregnancy testing kit

keep the child, have the child adopted or have an abortion.

Deciding to have an abortion can result in feelings of guilt and anxiety, even if the girl is sure she wants one (see chapter 7). Having a baby at a very young age is often very difficult. The girl may not have much support from other people. Her school or college career may be disrupted. She may not have a home of her own and may have very little money. Despite what some of the tabloid newspapers say, being a young mother, either living with a partner or on her own, is often little fun. Many young women become depressed and isolated, and their babies may not be adequately cared for.

## PREGNANCY TESTS

If a girl thinks she is pregnant and does not want to be she needs to act quickly. The first step is to get a pregnancy test. Tests can be done at your doctor's, a family planning clinic, a chemist who performs tests or clinics such as Brook Advisory or the British Pregnancy Advisory Service. There are also kits that can be bought from chemists to carry out tests at home.

## MYTHS ABOUT PREGNANCY

A surprising number of young people are not clear about exactly when and how a girl can become pregnant. There are still so many myths and misunderstandings. For example, many young people still think that a girl cannot get pregnant if she has intercourse during her period, if it is her first time, if she

though as many Dutch girls have intercourse as girls in this country. The difference is that more Dutch teenage girls use contraception effectively.

Having an unwanted pregnancy when you are a teenager can result in enormous pressures and difficulties. Some teenage girls who become pregnant may at first feel pleased to discover they can have children, but many panic when they start thinking about the reality of the situation. Who can they tell, what will they say to them and what are they going to do? Many young girls at first try to ignore their pregnancy and pretend it is not happening. Telling parents, boyfriends, other friends and the school can be very difficult. Eventually the girl concerned will have to decide whether she wants to

A teenage mother with her baby

## Emergency contraception

If a woman has had unprotected intercourse and thinks she could become pregnant she can do something about it as long as she acts quickly. Emergency contraception (the 'Morning After' pill) can be obtained from doctors and family planning clinics. If taken within 72 hours (three days) of unprotected intercourse, emergency contraception can ensure the woman does not become pregnant.

66 **When I told my mum, she went mad. She said "You've ruined my life. How could you do this?" Everyone was talking about who would pay for the abortion, but nobody asked me about it. I wasn't allowed to see my boyfriend. It was a terrible time.** 99

Emma, who became pregnant at 15

does not have an orgasm, if a man withdraws his penis from her vagina before ejaculating ('coming'), if she has a bath or washes out her vagina afterwards, has intercourse standing up, and so on.

Surveys show that teenagers today are more likely to use contraception than was the case in the 1960s or 1970s. However, many do not use contraception when they first start to have intercourse. This may be because of ignorance, feeling embarrassed, being drunk or high on drugs or the fact that

## Question
'Men do not take enough responsibility for contraception.' What do you think?

> ❝ You wouldn't think he was lovely if you'd been with him at three o'clock this morning. He's a full-time job and there's no one around to take him off my hands when it all gets too much. ❞
>
> Lisa, a 15-year-old single mother, talking about her baby *The Independent*, 1994

> ❝ My boyfriend and I were 15 when I fell pregnant. I couldn't believe it. You never think it's going to happen to you. I had so many plans... That's all gone now.' ❞
>
> A teenage single mother

are not used. Some, such as herpes and hepatitis, can be transmitted through oral sex, such as licking a man's penis, sucking a woman's clitoris or licking someone's anus. Pubic lice, warts and trich can be passed on by body contact.

How do you know if you have an STD? Whilst some STDs have no symptoms, many have similar symptoms. Common symptoms include unusual vaginal discharge in women and an abnormal discharge from the penis in men. Symptoms common to men and women include pain when urinating, a burning feeling or sores around the genitals, itching in the pubic hair and itching or a discharge from the anus.

If left untreated some STDs can cause serious problems including infertility in women. It is important to go to a GUM (Genito-Urinary Medicine) clinic if you think you could have an STD. The clinic will carry out blood, urine and swab tests to find out which STD you have. They will then be in a position to give treatment. Most STDs can be treated with antibiotics and some respond to creams.

sex was not planned. Many girls only go to the doctor or family planning clinic months after they have started having intercourse. Many boys fail to take any responsibility for contraception.

## SEXUALLY TRANSMITTED DISEASES

There are many diseases which can be caught from another person during sexual activity. They include chlamydia, gonorrhoea, genital warts, genital herpes, hepatitis, pubic lice (crabs), syphilis, thrush, trichomonas (trich) and HIV, the virus that eventually leads to AIDS. Most STDs (sexually transmitted diseases) can be passed from person to person through vaginal or anal intercourse where condoms

## CERVICAL CANCER

Cervical cancer is a cancer that attacks the cervix, the neck of the womb at the top of a woman's vagina. No one is sure exactly how it is caused but medical research suggests it has something to do with sexually transmitted viruses. The best way of protecting against cervical cancer is to use condoms when having intercourse. Women should also regularly have a 'smear test' which can give an early warning of cancerous cells. If detected early on treatment for cervical cancer is very successful.

# HIV AND AIDS

HIV is the virus that eventually leads to AIDS. The virus can be present in many body fluids but can only be transmitted from one person to another through blood, sperm or vaginal secretions. The most risky sexual activities when it comes to HIV are vaginal and anal intercourse without using a condom. Anal intercourse is usually more risky than vaginal intercourse because the anus tears more easily, making blood-to-blood contact more likely.

HIV stands for Human Immuno-Deficiency Virus. It is a virus that damages the immune system, making the body vulnerable to many diseases which it can usually resist. AIDS stands for Acquired Immune Deficiency Syndrome. It is the name given to a collection of medical conditions which eventually occur as a consequence of having HIV. You cannot 'catch AIDS' but you can become infected with HIV which in time will lead to AIDS. (For more information on HIV testing see chapter 7 of this book.)

HIV and AIDS has mainly affected gay men but it is also an issue for heterosexual men and women. Of the 11,500 people diagnosed as having AIDS in September 1995, over 90 per cent were men and less than 10 per cent were women. One per cent involved people who were infected during blood transfusions, six per cent involved sharing drug-injecting equipment and one per cent mother-to-child transmission. The percentage of gay or bisexual men infected by having anal intercourse with other men has been falling whilst the percentage of heterosexual transmissions has been rising. Research also indicates that where one partner is infected, transmission of HIV is more likely male to female than female to male. This means that heterosexual women may be at more risk than heterosexual men.

# MAKING CHOICES

Minimising the risks from having sex means planning, being careful about what you actually do with another person and making sure you do not do things that you do not wish to. This is what safer sex is all about.

It is not a good idea to be involved in sexual activity until you are sure that you want to. Some people suggest that young people should be encouraged to say no to sex and remain celibate. In America, this has led to campaigns to get young people to make a 'virginity pledge' and say they will not have sex until they are married. Other people regard this as unrealistic.

It is often assumed that sex equals

> **"** AIDS is a worldwide phenomenon. The World Health Organisation estimates that there are about two million people worldwide who have AIDS and about 12 million infected with HIV. **"**

**Question**
'It is not proper sex if you don't have intercourse.' What do you think?

having intercourse. One way of avoiding many of the risks associated with sex is to be sexual without having intercourse. Sexual activities such as mutual masturbation, oral sex, stroking and deep kissing can be used as alternatives to intercourse. A danger is that some young people may see these activities as a prelude to intercourse rather than enjoying them in their own right. Some may get 'carried away' and end up having unprotected intercourse. However, young people who communicate with their partner and are clear about what they want can be involved in a whole range of sexual activities without having intercourse.

## CONTRACEPTION

If young people choose to have intercourse, there are ways they can protect themselves from unwanted pregnancy, STDs and HIV. Whilst there are many different forms of contraception, none are ideal. Perhaps the most effective method for young people are to use both the female pill and male condoms. The pill can be obtained through family doctors, family planning clinics and agencies such as Brook Advisory. It is free and can be prescribed to under 16s without parental consent if the young girl is

The pill and condoms – the most effective contraceptives for young people

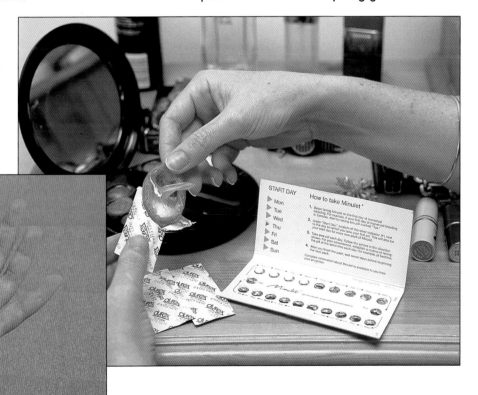

Norplant implants are inserted in the arm under the skin.

sufficiently mature and does not want her parents to know. (See chapter 5 for more on helping services.) Effective use of the pill involves understanding how it works, taking it regularly and having regular medical check ups. Although it is very effective in preventing pregnancy it does not protect against STDs and HIV.

The coil (intrauterine device or IUD) is rarely given to young women because of the risk of pelvic infections, which can lead to infertility. The diaphragm (or cap), sponge and female condom can all be difficult to place properly in the vagina and can be a bit messy. They tend to be used by women who are more experienced with sex and confident enough about their bodies to use them properly.

Natural (or rhythm) methods involve avoiding intercourse at times when a woman is most fertile. The woman has to keep a chart of her periods and carefully plan when to have intercourse and when to avoid it. Even done properly it is not a very reliable method. Injections like Depo Prevera or Noristerat can provide up to three months' protection but are not usually recommended for younger women. In America, Norplant is the latest contraceptive used by young people. Small rods containing a chemical contraceptive are put into the girl's arm. Norplant can provide up to five years of

protection, but it can have unpleasant side effects.

Another drawback to all these contraceptives is that none, apart from the condom, protect young people from STDs and HIV. (For more information about contraception, see the Helpline and Further Reading lists on pages 59 and 60.)

Condoms are an effective form of contraception if used correctly and also protect against STDs and HIV. They are essential for heterosexual couples who have vaginal or anal intercourse and gay men who have anal intercourse. Stronger condoms are recommended for anal intercourse. Condoms can be bought from chemists and vending machines but can also be obtained free from family planning clinics. They need to be used carefully if they are to be effective.

Safer sex can be about not having sex, avoiding intercourse or using contraceptives (especially condoms) if you do have intercourse. Above all it is about being assertive, knowing what you want and talking and negotiating with your partner. Too often young people (and many older people as well) have sex without communicating with their partner. Some people feel too embarrassed to talk openly. Talking openly, being clear about what you want and finding different ways to enjoy yourself is the key to safer sex.

**Question**
If a young person does not want to have sex but is under pressure from his/her partner to do so, what should the young person say and do?

**Find out!**
What does a man need to do, and avoid doing, to make sure he uses condoms properly?

# WHAT ARE THE LAWS RELATING TO SEX?

Young people may not realise that as recently as 30 years ago it was very difficult to get a divorce, abortion was only allowed in exceptional circumstances, contraception was not freely available and homosexuality was illegal. What are the main laws relating to sex in Britain today, how do they affect young people and are they sensible laws?

The law states that at 18 young people have the right to vote and can get married without parental consent. (Until 1969 you had to be 21 years old to marry without parental consent.) At 16 young people can marry if their parents agree and they have the right to consent to their own medical treatment. This includes the right to obtain contraception or an abortion without parental consent. However, some laws are different in Scotland and Northern Ireland and in England and Wales. For example, in Northern Ireland

There are many laws that relate to young people and sex.

young people have to be 17 years old to consent to their own medical treatment or legally have intercourse and abortion is not as freely available as in other parts of the United Kingdom.

Doctors may prescribe contraceptives to a girl under 16 if it is believed she is sufficiently mature, understands the consequences and it is in her best interests (see chapter 5). Abortion is not available on demand but only in certain circumstances (see chapter 7 ).

One of the main laws regulating young people's sexual behaviour concerns the age of consent. It is an offence for a male (in law a boy aged 14 years or over) to have intercourse with a girl under 16 years of age. The girl is not acting illegally but the man is and he could be taken to court and if found guilty fined and/or imprisoned. It is not illegal for a woman to have sexual intercourse with a male under 16 years of age although it is possible that she could be charged with the offence of indecent assault.

It is illegal for men to be involved in homosexual acts together if one of them is under 18 years of age. (This law has recently been changed from 21 years of age.) For example, if two men aged 19 and 17 years old have a homosexual relationship, the 19-year-old could be prosecuted and even sent to jail. Gay relationships are also banned in the armed forces and have resulted in a number of men and women being dismissed.

## NEW LAWS

The government passed a law in 1988 which made it illegal for local authorities to 'intentionally promote homosexuality' or 'promote the teaching in a maintained school of the acceptability of homosexuality as a pretended family relationship'. This law is called Section 28 and does not apply to individual schools or teachers but to the actions of local authority officers. As of 1996 it has never been used to take anyone to court and according to lawyers is never likely to be used because of the difficulty in proving that 'promotion' actually took place.

There are also new laws about the teaching of sex education in schools. In 1994 a new law was introduced which said that all maintained secondary schools had to have a sex education programme, although the law did not specify what that programme should consist of. In private and primary schools it is left to the school authorities or governors to decide whether there should be a sex education programme. References to sex and HIV/AIDS were taken out of the compulsory National Curriculum and parents were given the legal right to remove their children from sex education lessons. (For more details see chapter 8.)

There are many other laws relating to sex. Laws have changed to give police and social service departments more powers to investigate cases of child sexual abuse. The law on rape was changed in 1991 so that a man can now be charged with raping his wife. Laws relating to indecent assault, indecent exposure and sexual harassment can be used for situations where consent to sex has not been given. There are also laws relating to pornography and obscene publications (magazines, videos etc). Laws relating to prostitution include those of soliciting, living off immoral earnings and kerb crawling.

Break-time at a secondary school. For many of the subjects that these boys will study, there are detailed programmes of work. But new laws about sex education are not specific about what must be taught.

# THE AGE OF CONSENT

Even though it is illegal for a man to have intercourse with a girl who is under 16 (even if she consents), many young people break this law. Surveys show that about one third of girls in the United Kingdom have had intercourse by the age of 16. It is rare that the law is used to prosecute men who have intercourse with under-16 girls. Where it is used it usually involves a man who is a lot older than the girl and/or where the girl herself or her parents complain to the police. In most situations a boy or young man who has consenting intercourse with his 15-year-old girlfriend would not be charged.

Other countries in Europe have different ages of consent. Whilst the age of consent for heterosexual sex is still 18 in Malta and Turkey and 17 in Northern Ireland and Eire, it is 16 in Belgium, Finland, Italy and Norway, Portugal and Switzerland. In Czechoslovakia, Denmark, France, Poland and Sweden it is 15 years old. In Austria, Bulgaria, Germany and Hungary it is 14 and in Spain it is 12.

This does not mean that men who have intercourse with girls under 16 years old will not be prosecuted. For example, in the Netherlands the age of consent laws work so it is not automatically an offence for a man to have intercourse with a girl who is over

## Question
**Does the law about the age of consent need changing?**

12 years old. Where a 12 - 16 year old girl consents to intercourse the man can be prosecuted if the girl or her parents complain to the police that the man has taken advantage of her or put undue pressure on her. The Netherlands deals with the issue of the age of consent in this way to protect young girls whilst at the same time meaning large numbers of young people are not breaking the law.

## THE DEBATE

Many people in this country still prefer to keep the present law rather than lower the age of consent. They stress that having sex under 16 is too young and that girls need protecting, particularly from older men. Large and increasing numbers of young people have intercourse under the age of 16 and ignore the law. Those in favour of lowering

the age of consent say that telling under-16s not to have sex seems to have little, if any, impact on what they do. They argue that knowing they are breaking the law may make under-16s and their partners more secretive about having sex and mean they are less likely to talk to adults about it, and reluctant to seek out contraceptive advice and help when needed. In other words the law as it stands may contribute to the high teenage pregnancy rate and incidence of STDs and HIV.

Discussion of the age of consent for consenting homosexuals is often even more heated. Whilst the government has recently reduced the age from 21 years old to 18 many people believe it should be 16 years, the same as for heterosexuals. Nearly all other European countries (apart from Austria, Hungary and

## Question

'The age of consent for gay men should be the same age as for heterosexuals. What do you think?'

A march calling for equal rights for gay people

Liechtenstein) put the age of consent for gay
men at the same age as for heterosexuals.
Until recently the United Kingdom had the
highest age of consent for gay men in the
whole of Europe, apart from Cyprus where
sex between men is still illegal at any age.

People who oppose equality for gay men
have focused their arguments on the issues
of protecting young men on the one hand
and denying them the right to be sexual as
they wish to be on the other hand. They
believe young men are often pressurised into
gay sex by older men when they do not
really want to be involved, and they tend to
be 'against' homosexuality. Others argue
that the present law forces young gay men to
hide their true sexuality and feelings and
makes them reluctant to seek out helping
services when they need them, which does
not help in preventing the spread of STDs or
HIV amongst gay men.

## WHAT IS THE PURPOSE OF THE LAW?

The laws relating to sex should aim to
protect people, especially young people, from
the unwanted advances of others. Laws
relating to sexual abuse, rape, indecent
assault, indecent exposure and sexual
harassment are supported by nearly
everyone. However, other laws are hotly
debated because they prohibit mutually
consenting sexual behaviour.

One view is that the law should only enter
where there is not true consent between
people, where there is not full responsibility
on the part of one or more of the people
involved (such as children) or where offence
is caused to other people who have
witnessed the event or been involved against
their will.

If the law is not to be used to attempt to
force the morals of one group on other
people who do not share their views, we
have to learn to be tolerant towards others
who choose to be involved in sexual acts that
we may not approve of for ourselves. We
also need to take account of the actual
impact of different laws (both positive and
negative), whether on balance they are a
good thing and whether they would be
respected by people.

## THE LAWS ON PROSTITUTION

Prostitution involves the exchange of sex for
money. Most, but not all, involves women
prostitutes and male customers. Current
laws do not seem to stop prostitution. They
may have the effect of women (rather than
their male customers) being fined and then
going back on the streets to get money to
pay the fines. The law may also mean
women are less likely to seek out medical
help when needed and more likely to contract
and spread STDs and HIV. Many people have
suggested the best way of reducing
prostitution is to provide better employment

Laws against prostitution seem to have little impact on reducing it.

opportunities for women. Similar things could be said about male prostitution and rent boys. Countries like the Netherlands and Germany and some American states have 'legalised' prostitution for these reasons and encouraged licensing, health checks, use of condoms etc. in an attempt to control prostitution and protect both prostitutes and clients.

## CONCLUSION

The laws related to sex are constantly changing and will continue to do so in the future. In the 1960s and 1970s many laws were passed which gave people greater freedom and more rights to make their own decisions. The 1980s and 1990s have seen a return to some laws which some people feel attempt to enforce morals rather than protect people. New laws restrict the support local authorities can give to gay people, limit school sex education, restrict women's rights to abortion and censor sexually explicit images on television and in videos, films and magazines. The debate on how far such measures are justified will continue.

### Question
'If people consent to sexual acts together it is no business of the law what they do.' What do you think?

### Question
If you could change one law relating to sexual behaviour what would you change and why?

# WHAT HELPING SERVICES DO YOUNG PEOPLE NEED?

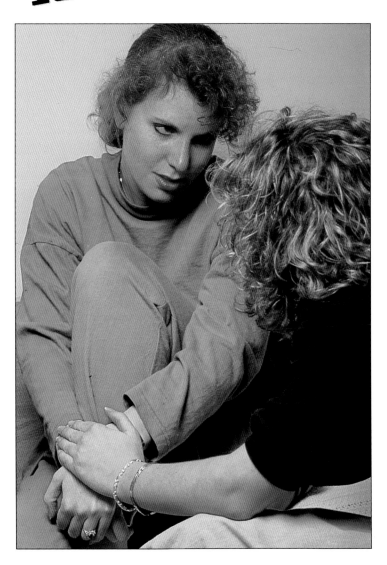

A young woman being counselled at a clinic

People all over the world have used 'home-made' barrier forms of contraception for thousands of years. However, it was not until 1921 that the first family planning clinic in the United Kingdom opened in London. Condoms were first manufactured on a large scale in 1932 and were mainly on sale to men in some barber shops. Boots chemist shops did not sell them until 1965 because the company felt they were associated with 'promiscuity, vice and prostitution'. Many couples did not use any contraceptives, other than withdrawal or abstaining from sex.

It was not until the 1960s that family planning clinics became widespread in this country. The services offered were limited and usually were only for married or engaged women. Some clinics would not give contraceptives unless women brought along their marriage certificate. In 1974, the pill became more widely available to both married and unmarried women free on the National Health.

## CONTRACEPTIVE SERVICES

In 1991 more than 22,000 under-16s (mainly girls) went to a family planning clinic in England. However, it was also estimated that less than half the under-16 girls who were having intercourse had sought contraception from a clinic or family doctor.

Research suggests that many young people do not know where their local family planning clinic is. In one recent survey of 14-18 year olds in Cheshire only half knew where their local clinic was and these were mainly the 17 and 18-year-olds.

Many young people feel embarrassed about the prospect of going to a clinic or their doctor for contraceptives. A major reason why young people do not go is that they fear that the service will not be confidential. They may worry about who will see them there, but also worry that the staff may tell their parents. Many do not realise that if they are under 16 years of age most doctors will NOT inform their parents.

## CONFIDENTIALITY

Young people under the age of 16 can obtain contraceptives and other health services from their family doctor or clinics without their parents being informed. Recent guidance for doctors and nurses has

### Find out!
Find out what sexual health services exist for young people in your locality. What services do they provide?

stressed that:
- The duty of confidentiality owed to a person under 16 is as great as that owed to any other person.
- Any competent young person, regardless of age, can independently seek medical advice and give valid consent to medical treatment.
- Doctors and nurses need to consider what is in the patient's best interest, regardless of their age.

Doctors and nurses will usually encourage under-16s to talk to their parents, but most will not press the issue if the young person concerned is clear that he/she cannot talk to his/her parents. Medical staff will also usually not just talk about contraception but wider issues about sexual relationships and feelings.

## WHAT SORT OF SERVICES?

Most recent surveys about the sort of sexual health services young people want have reached similar conclusions. In one survey,16 to19-year-olds wanted
- a range of sexual health services specially for young people
- contraception and contraceptive advice
- provision for counselling and advice on sexual problems and unwanted pregnancy
- pregnancy testing
- advice on sexually transmitted diseases
- cervical smear tests

- information and advice on general health matters such as diet and drug use.

The young people also sought
- doctors and medical staff to be friendly and non-judgemental
- younger staff aged 20 to 40 years old
- a choice of male or female staff. Girls felt this was more important than boys. Many girls said they preferred to see a woman.
- confidentiality. When asked who their first choice was to obtain advice on sexual matters, about 40 per cent said a family planning clinic, 35 per cent a family doctor and only about 10 per cent said a parent or a friend.
- services that were conveniently located with accessible opening hours. Saturday mornings were the most popular opening times.
- a friendly, welcoming, relaxed atmosphere and decor appropriate to young people, with drinks and magazines available.
- 'drop in' rather than appointment service.

It was suggested that the service should be advertised in a variety of ways including on TV, leaflets, information in school, posters and billboards, newspapers and magazines.

There were some additional differences between what girls and boys wanted. Whilst a majority of girls preferred attending family planning clinics, more boys preferred going to their family doctor for advice on sexual matters. To actually obtain contraceptives, boys tended to use chemists and vending machines to get condoms whilst girls used family planning clinics and doctors to obtain the pill.

Some surveys have also suggested separate clinics for young women and young men, and opening times just after the school or college day ends. A few have even

suggested contraception should be available within school, but this has been seen as very controversial.

## VIEWS ON CONTRACEPTION

A key question is whether making contraception more easily available to under-16s actually encourages them to have intercourse. The evidence suggests that it does not. We know that over half under-16s do not use contraceptives when they first have intercourse. We also know that in countries which have better access to contraception for young people (such as the Netherlands and Sweden) there are not more young people having intercourse at a younger age than in Britain. The evidence suggests that most under-16s who have intercourse will do so whether contraceptives are available or not.

Different religions have different views about contraception. The officials of the Roman Catholic church are opposed to the use of any contraception other than natural methods involving avoiding intercourse when women are most fertile. Despite this, many Catholics use contraceptives. The Church of England allows people to make their own choices about contraception. Amongst Hindus use of contraception is often acceptable after the birth of a son. Islam allows contraception where there is already a very young child or where there is fear for the physical or mental well-being of the mother. Vasectomy amongst men is strictly forbidden but female sterilisation is allowed in some cases. Sikhism does not outlaw contraception but encouragement of large families has often meant contraception is not used. This is gradually changing with acceptance of smaller families. Contraception is widely used amongst Jews but some very religious Jews believe that it should only be used if pregnancy would put a woman at significant physical or mental risk.

## TALKING TO PARENTS

In a 1994 survey of girls aged 13 to 18 years old, 'Mizz' magazine found that nearly 80 per cent said they would not talk to their parents before using contraception. The reasons given for not talking to parents were being scared of their reaction, wanting to keep it a secret and feeling too embarrassed. Obviously a lot more needs to be done to encourage young people and parents to talk openly about such issues.

> " Youngsters having sex is a fact of life... and while society has mixed feelings about the issue we cannot close our eyes to it. We must help young people, not sweep the issue under the carpet. "
>
> Dr Meera Kishen *Sunday Times* 1994

## LOOKING TO THE FUTURE

In public the government advises that young people should be dissuaded from having sex. At the same time they know that many young people ignore this advice. They have set targets in their 'Health of the Nation' strategy to reduce teenage pregnancies by 50 per cent by the year 2000, and to reduce

Most parents and children find it difficult to talk openly about sex.

sexually transmitted diseases and HIV. To achieve this they know that more young people need to be encouraged to use sexual health services. This has led to many Health Authorities recently setting up special young people's sexual health clinics.

A number of these services are run by Brook Advisory. There are now more than 25 Brook Centres in Britain. Doctors, nurses and counsellors give information and advice about a whole range of sexual matters, prescribe the pill, give out condoms, do pregnancy tests, prescribe emergency contraception, carry out cervical cancer smears, support young women who are pregnant and wish to keep their babies and help those who wish to have an abortion. The service is free and confidential. Some health centres and family doctors have opened special young people's clinics. Some

> ## " The aims of Brook
> The prevention and mitigation of the suffering caused by unwanted pregnancy by educating young persons in matters of sex and contraception and developing among them a sense of responsibility in regard to sexual behaviour "

youth clubs have teamed up with Health Services to house clinics at times which are convenient to young people. After school, early evenings and weekends have been found to be good times.

This Dutch youth club has a sexual health clinic as well as the usual youth club activities.

Some colleges and universities have begun to offer such services for their students. A number of people have suggested that this should also happen in secondary schools and although this is now happening in some States in America it is regarded as too controversial in this country. The last few years have also seen the development of telephone help lines focusing on sex issues.

Most sexual health services are targeted at young women. If young men are involved it is usually by going along with their girlfriends. However, young men have an important role to play in obtaining and using contraceptives and have their own concerns about sex. Some new services are experimenting with 'Men only' clinics both to encourage more young men to come forward and because some young women say they prefer 'women only' services.

Services for young gay men and women have not been as well resourced. Most have been organised and run on a voluntary basis by gay people themselves. They now include some telephone help lines and local support groups. Large cities often have gay centres offering information and advice, social activities, support groups and a place to meet other gay people. The advent of HIV and AIDS and the fact that gay men were the first to be directly affected has also led to more advice, information and support for young gay people.

Services for young people are improving but more needs to be done, especially in rural areas. Some people still see the development of services as a bad thing but they are a dwindling minority. The future will see more services developed. It will be important for young people to be involved in deciding what type of services they want. It will also be important to advertise such services widely so that more young people are aware of their existence.

## Question
'Contraceptives should be available in secondary schools.' What do you think?

## Question
'Young people should be encouraged not to have sex rather than use contraceptive services.' What do you think?

# IS IT A GOOD IDEA TO HAVE AN HIV TEST?

Many people think there is a test for AIDS. In fact there is no test for AIDS. There is a blood test that can detect the antibodies to HIV, the virus that eventually leads to AIDS. If someone 'tests positive' it means that they have the antibodies and also have HIV.

When people feel they have put themselves at risk of contracting HIV through unsafe sexual practices (such as vaginal or anal intercourse without using condoms) or sharing drug-injecting equipment, they may think about whether to have an HIV test. The decision about whether to take the test or not can be a very difficult one. (For more information about HIV and AIDS see chapter 3.)

## WHAT DOES THE TEST INVOLVE?

The HIV test can be obtained through your doctor. There are also clinics which specialise in HIV and AIDS, but most are for all sexually transmitted diseases (STDs). They are called GUM (Genito Urinary Medicine) clinics and many large hospitals have them. Some testing kits which can be used at home are now available.

The test involves taking a sample of blood, usually from the arm. The sample is tested for the presence of HIV antibodies. It used to take up to three weeks to get the result back but some clinics now give the result on the same day.

The test is not 100 per cent accurate. About one per cent of tests show an inaccurate result. For this reason two blood samples are usually taken. How soon the test is done after possible infection is also an important factor. The antibodies to HIV can often only be detected a few months after infection. This is called the 'window period'. If someone is tested soon after becoming infected the result might still be negative. Another test would be needed a few months later.

Most doctors and clinics will not test people without arranging for counselling both before and after the test. They will want to be

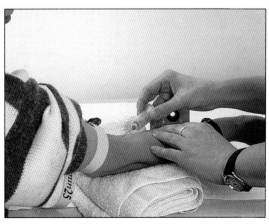

The HIV test involves having a blood test.

sure that people who go for a test are clear about why they want to be tested, what it involves and the possible implications of having a positive or negative result.

As HIV is such a sensitive issue doctors and clinics try to ensure confidentiality and make sure no one else knows about it. Some medical staff may be reluctant to test an under-16 without the parents being involved. However, others will go ahead without parental consent if they think the young person is mature enough, understands the issues involved and that parents knowing could make matters worse.

## TEST RESULTS

A positive test result means that a person has HIV and could be infectious to other

people if they practise unsafe sex or share drug-injecting equipment. It does not mean that they will infect other people by normal, everyday contact, kissing or practising safer sex. It also does not mean they have got AIDS. AIDS is diagnosed by the presence of various medical conditions. Almost everyone who has HIV goes on to get AIDS but this can take many years. Recent reports have suggested some people with HIV may be alive and healthy 20 years later and that the average time between first being infected with HIV and getting full blown AIDS is 10 to 12 years. This also means that many people who have HIV and have not been for a test may have no idea that they have it.

A negative test result means (taking into account the 'window period') that a person does not have HIV at that time. It does not mean that a person will not become infected in future if they later put themselves at risk.

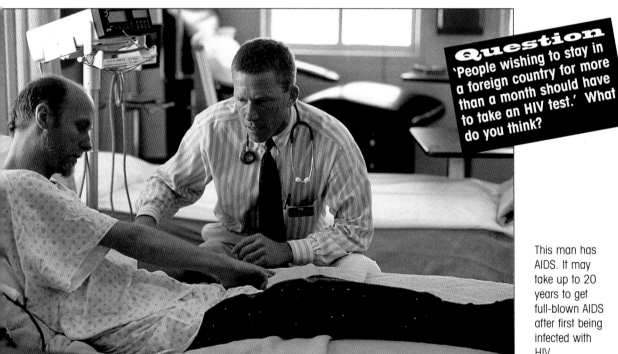

**Question**
'People wishing to stay in a foreign country for more than a month should have to take an HIV test.' What do you think?

This man has AIDS. It may take up to 20 years to get full-blown AIDS after first being infected with HIV.

HIV can be passed from mother to baby but it only happens in 10 to 20 per cent of cases where the mother is infected.

## SOME REASONS FOR TAKING THE TEST

Some people who feel they have put themselves at risk of getting HIV decide to take the test. Others decide that, even if they may have HIV, it is better not to know. The decision about whether or not to have a test can be very difficult and this is why it is very important that people have counselling beforehand to weigh up the pros and cons and decide what is best for them.

Some people are happier knowing for sure whether or not they have HIV. If they do not know they may worry all the time and find it difficult to get on with their life.

Getting a negative result would be a great relief.

Getting a positive result may enable people to start health checks and treatment earlier. Although there is no cure for HIV or AIDS, certain medical treatments may help slow down the progression of HIV to full-blown AIDS. A positive test may also mean they can alter their lifestyle so that it is healthier. This can be important because HIV involves a breakdown of the body's immune system, decreasing resistance to common infections.

Some people take a test because they want to reassure their partner and be clear about exactly what they will do in their sexual relationships. If they have a positive test they will know that practising safer sex is crucial if they are not to infect other people. If they have a negative test, and their partner is also negative, they may not need to practise safer sex.

The issue of having children can also affect decisions about whether or not to have a test. We know that HIV can be passed from mother to baby during pregnancy and that this happens in 10 to 20 per cent of cases where a pregnant woman has HIV. If a woman thinks she could have HIV and is thinking of having children she may wish to have a test for that reason. This will also be an issue for men who wish to become fathers and are concerned that they could have HIV. The danger is that they could infect their female partner and she could then infect her baby.

# SOME REASONS FOR NOT TAKING THE TEST

Many people take the test in the hope that the result will be negative, but what if it is positive? They may react to the news by feeling intense shock, anger and depression. They may feel they have been sentenced to death and find no point in living (even though many people respond in more positive ways and decide to live life to the full). Some people have committed suicide after finding out they have HIV. This is why having counselling after getting the result ('post-test' counselling) is so important. It is also why many people decide not to have a test. They feel that they would be better not knowing about whether they have HIV. They

**Question**
If you had put yourself at risk of contracting HIV, would you go for a test and why/ why not?

can get on with their life and can still practise safer sex to protect other people and themselves in future.

It is very common for people who have HIV to suffer discrimination in many areas of their lives. They may face rejection by partners, friends and family and find themselves isolated. People with HIV have also faced harassment, abuse and discrimination from employers and work colleagues. Some people have been hounded out of their jobs or sacked by employers, although some large companies and organisations have taken steps to protect people who have HIV. You can see that one key issue for people who have an HIV test is who they tell about it. Many people will feel they need to keep the matter secret from many of the people they are close to because of the discrimination and rejection they may face. It can be very difficult and lonely having to cope with a positive test result without people close to you knowing.

Going for a test can also make it difficult to obtain life insurance (to provide for a partner or children when someone dies) or a mortgage to buy a house or flat. If someone has HIV, companies will not usually offer life insurance or grant a mortgage.

As you can see, the decision about whether or not to have an HIV test can be a very difficult one to make.

**Find out!**
What restrictions, if any, are put on employees in the food industry and public services regarding HIV and AIDS?

**Question**
What do you think can be done to reduce discrimination against people who have HIV?

# THE ABORTION DEBATE

Many people talk of a 'woman's right to choose' whether or not to have an abortion. Some even campaign for 'abortion on demand'. Others believe abortion should be outlawed. Some opponents even picket abortion clinics and try to stop women getting in. What are the facts about abortion and what are the arguments used to justify and oppose it?

Up to 1968 abortion was legal in Britain only where there was a danger that a pregnant woman would die or where continuing the pregnancy would seriously threaten her health. Many illegal 'back street' abortions, as many as 100,000 a year, were carried out, often by people with few medical qualifications and in unhygienic situations.

Today, abortion is legal where two doctors agree that a woman is less than 24 weeks pregnant AND that

1 continuing the pregnancy would involve risk to her physical or mental health greater than if the pregnancy were terminated

OR

2 continuing the pregnancy would involve risk to the physical or mental health of any existing children in her family.

Doctors can take into account the woman's financial, family and housing situation as well as her available emotional support both currently and in the foreseeable future.

Reading the instructions on a home pregnancy testing kit

> " In Britian, about one in six women now aged between 16 and 60 have had an abortion. "

The 24-week limit does not apply where continuing the pregnancy would put the woman's life at risk, or seriously and permanently damage her physical or mental health, or result in a child being born with a serious handicap.

Most abortions are performed under the clause about risk to the physical or mental health of the woman. In 1991 89 per cent of abortions in the United Kingdom were for that reason. A further 10 per cent were due to risk to existing children and under one per cent due to risk of the child being born seriously handicapped or risk to the life of the woman.

To obtain an abortion on the National Health Service a woman has to obtain the signature of two doctors. There is no simple right to have an abortion. Some doctors who feel women should be able to make up their own minds interpret the law widely and will grant an abortion to most women who want one. Other doctors refuse to agree to women having abortions and interpret the law very strictly. This means that some women have to go to great lengths to find two doctors who will grant an abortion.

Some areas of the country provide good abortion services under the Health Service but others do not. Less than half of all abortions in Britain are performed under the Health Service, with the rest being privately

### Question
**If you were drafting an abortion law for this country what would it say?**

paid for. (A private abortion usually costs between £200 and £500.) The percentage of abortions performed under the Health Service varies from 90 per cent in Scotland to under 30 per cent in some areas of Britain.

## ABORTION LAWS IN OTHER COUNTRIES

In most European countries, and in Canada, China and Australia, abortion is legally available on broad medical and social grounds as it is in Britain. In the Irish Republic abortion is outlawed in nearly every circumstance. In Northern Ireland it is restricted to extreme circumstances where the mother's life is at risk from continuing pregnancy. The situation is similar in many South American countries and in parts of Africa and the Far East. In America, although abortion is supposed to be legally available, pressure from anti-abortionists and the fact that most abortions have to be paid for has meant that in some states it is very difficult to get an abortion, especially if you are poor. Women from countries where abortion is illegal may visit another country to obtain an abortion legally.

## HOW ARE ABORTIONS PERFORMED?

There are a number of ways in which legal, medical abortions are carried out, depending on the number of weeks women are pregnant. The longer into pregnancy, the

This Dutch poster asks 'Unwanted pregnancy – what now?' It offers help for mother and unborn child.

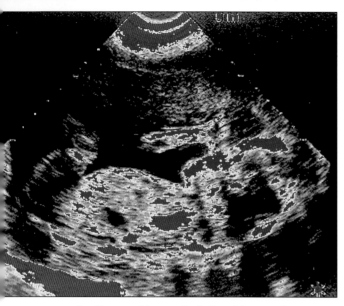

An ultra sound image of a foetus at four months

more complicated abortion becomes.

Recently an abortion pill called RU486 has been introduced in this country. It can be used up to nine weeks into pregnancy and involves taking three pills and using a tablet placed in the vagina. It results in bleeding like a heavy period. RU 486 is relatively new and not very widely available yet.

Up to 12 weeks of pregnancy the most common method of abortion is vacuum aspiration. The contents of the uterus are sucked out through a thin tube using an electric pump. It is usually done under a general anaesthetic.

Between 12 and 16 weeks of pregnancy abortion is usually carried out by dilating (opening) the woman's cervix and removing the contents of the womb using an instrument. This also involves a general anaesthetic.

After 16 weeks of pregnancy the methods used are more complicated and distressing. Hormones are used to cause a miscarriage and the woman either has to go through labour or undergo an operation similar to a caesarian section.

Legal abortion is very safe, especially when it is carried out early in pregnancy. In fact many more women die in childbirth than from having legal abortions.

After having an abortion many women feel a huge relief but they may also feel sadness and guilt. Some may even feel very depressed. Having someone to talk to and provide support can be very Important.

## MAKING THE DECISION

There are many reasons why women decide they do not wish to continue with a pregnancy. Some may feel they are too young to be responsible for a child and that they have not got the means to provide a child with a decent home. Women who become pregnant outside a stable relationship may feel unable to bring up a child on their own.

> **❝ We debate the morality of abortion, yet we belittle the problems women can face as mothers... When motherhood is unexpected or unprepared for, it can still plunge a woman (and her child) into poverty and despair... It is time to stop blaming women for making difficult decisions that will affect their lives, alone. ❞**
>
> Kate Figes *The Guardian* January 1996

Others may feel they are too old to be a mother. Some may feel that pregnancy has come at the wrong time in their life and that they have too many other responsibilities or already have a number of children. Some women may feel that problems they have in their relationship or marriage make having a child extremely difficult. Many women who become pregnant through rape or sexual abuse will choose to have an abortion. There may also be reasons to do with physical health. The woman or her partner may have a hereditary disease which could be passed on to her baby. Tests may have shown that the baby is likely to be born with a serious disability. The woman may have a serious illness herself which could be made worse by going through pregnancy and childbirth.

Deciding whether or not to have an abortion can be extremely difficult. A woman needs to think clearly about the options available to her, her situation now and what it is likely to be in the future. It obviously helps if she can discuss it with her partner, if she has one, and her family and friends may help. She might also speak to a sympathetic family doctor or a doctor or counsellor at a Family Planning Clinic or agency such as the Brook Advisory or the British Pregnancy Advisory Service.

## THE ARGUMENTS AGAINST ABORTION

There are a number of organisations in Britain who actively campaign against abortion. The two main organisations are

An anti-abortion rally in the US

> **"** ...the death of a foetus is a real death. America's high rate of abortion - which ends more than a quarter of all pregnancies - can only be rightly understood as **"** a failure.
>
> Naomi Wolf *The Guardian* January 1996

LIFE and SPUC (Society to Protect the Unborn Child). They produce pamphlets and videos, and lobby MPs to have the law changed. They also offer support for women who choose not to have abortions and try to persuade pregnant women not to have an abortion. Some of their more militant members also hold demonstrations, and picket abortion clinics and contraceptive services for young people such as Brook Advisory.

Militant anti-abortion campaigners in America use violence as a way of trying to close down abortion clinics. They picket abortion clinics and harass and attack staff and women who go to them. Some clinics have been fire bombed, and at least four doctors working at abortion clinics have been shot dead. There have recently been concerns that some of these people are coming to Britain to persuade anti-abortion groups to use similar tactics here.

Anti-abortion campaigners say that abortion is murder. They believe that life begins at the moment of conception and that abortion should be outlawed even for cases where the woman has been raped, the child may be born seriously disabled or there is a risk that continuing the pregnancy will result in death of the mother.

LIFE and SPUC believe the availability of abortion encourages promiscuity and lowers respect for life. Many of their supporters are also against contraception. They say that many women are pressurised into abortion without really wanting to go through with it. They also say some women take the issue too lightly and use abortion as a convenient form of contraception. They stress the emotional and physical health dangers of abortion, including depression, and the possibility that having an abortion may make it more difficult for a woman to have a normal pregnancy if she later wants one.

Those against abortion believe that life is sacred and that women who do not want to keep their baby can always give them up for adoption.

## ABORTION AND RELIGIOUS BELIEFS

The Roman Catholic Church is the only major world religion to rule against abortion in all circumstances. The Church of England is generally against abortion but agrees to it being performed when continuing pregnancy would result in a serious risk to the health of the mother. Judaism, Hindu scriptures and Islam make a similar stand on abortion. The Free Churches - Baptist and Methodist - hold that abortion is a matter for the individual woman to decide and take social and emotional factors into consideration. These are

### Question
**When do you think life begins and how relevant do you think it is to the abortion debate?**

the 'official views' of religions based on what religious leaders have said. Many religious people have different views about abortion from those of their religious leaders. They may believe that women have a right to make their own decisions about abortion. Women of all religious backgrounds continue to seek abortions.

# THE RIGHT TO ABORTION

People who believe women should have a right to obtain an abortion emphasise that all children should be wanted children who can be loved and cared for. They believe women should not be forced to continue with pregnancy if they do not wish to and stress that abortion, especially early on in

pregnancy, involves less risk to a woman's physical and mental health than continuing with an unwanted pregnancy. They argue that the health and wellbeing of a woman and her existing family can be jeopardised if she is forced to continue with unwanted pregnancy. They say that women do not take the issue of abortion lightly and should be allowed to make such difficult decisions themselves without interference from others.

Pro-choice campaigners believe abortion may be especially necessary when a woman has been raped, subjected to sexual abuse or knows that a pregnancy will result in a seriously handicapped child. They also believe abortion may be necessary when the woman is very young or much older. Pregnancy and having a child may be particularly damaging to such women and

A pro-abortion rally in Washington, USA

> **Not only did generations of women throw themselves down stairs, drink gin and soak in boiling hot baths, they used iron hooks, coat hangers and took drugs and other poisons in an attempt to abort their babies. Those who could not face the prospect bore their children and then smothered them or disposed of them by some other means, claiming they had died in childbirth'.**
>
> Wendy Holden *Unlawful Carnage Knowledge*
> Harper Collins 1994

result in children who are not properly cared for.

Supporters of the right to abortion also take issue with the idea that life begins at conception. They argue that a new person does not exist until the foetus is capable of surviving independently of its mother's body and that the foetus is 'potential' life. They also stress that nature chooses not to allow all fertilised eggs to develop. As many as 15 to 20 per cent of confirmed pregnancies end in miscarriage.

Above all, pro-choice campaigners believe that women will seek out abortions whether it is legal or not. They point out that where

abortion is illegal, back-street abortions are used and this leads to severe health problems and a significant increase in deaths amongst pregnant women. For them, the issue is not one of whether individual women should have an abortion or not, it is a question of freedom of choice.

## Question

There have been cases where men have gone to court to try to stop their wives having an abortion. Should men have any say in the issue and if so what?

# SEX EDUCATION AND OTHER ISSUES FOR YOUNG PEOPLE AND SCHOOLS

## MESSAGES ABOUT SEX

**Question**

Do young people's magazines encourage young people to have sex at an early age or are they an important source of sex education?

Children learn about sex from a very early age from their parents and other people around them. Even if they are not actually told much, or it is not openly discussed, children receive messages about sex. These messages may indicate

Teenage magazines are now the most common way young people get information about sex.

**Question**
What sex education have you and your friends had? Who has provided you with the best information?

# SCHOOL SEX EDUCATION

that sex is natural, pleasurable and can be openly discussed or that it is something to be ashamed of and not talked about.

Other messages come from the media. In contrast to 30 years ago young people are now bombarded with information about sex through the media. This, together with discussion amongst friends, is now probably the main source of information about sex for many young people. Despite recent attempts to improve the quality of sex education in schools many young people are critical of the sex education they receive. Most think they receive 'too little, too late' and that the sex education they do receive is not detailed enough and fails to address the realities of being a young person today.

A 1994 survey in Mizz magazine asked teenage girls where they got most of their information about sex from.
70% said magazines.
37% said their friends
25% said teachers at school.
19% said parents.
(Some chose more than one main source).

**Find out!**
What kinds of products use sex in their advertisements? Are such adverts effective or are they offensive? Do men and women have different views about this?

Good school sex education has many advantages over other sources of information. It is more likely to be accurate and relevant to young people. Teachers have the opportunity to tailor sex education to fit what their students need and want. Above all it can give young people the chance to openly discuss, learn and question. The problem is that there is not any agreement in this country about the role of sex education in schools.

The current government has recently made new laws controlling sex education in schools and issued guidance about the way it should be taught. The law now states that sex education should be provided in all 'maintained' secondary schools (those which come under Local Authority control). This means that sex education is not compulsory in private or state primary schools where the head or governors can decide whether or not sex education should be taught. The law also now states that key aspects of sex education (such as abortion, contraception and HIV/AIDS) should NOT be taught as part of the compulsory national curriculum. Sex education should mainly be taught in non compulsory areas of the curriculum such as

" Surveys show that boys tend to get less sex education than girls from their parents. "

Personal and Social Education. Parents have been given a legal right to withdraw their children from sex education lessons.

The government has not laid out what should be taught in sex education lessons other than that it should include something about HIV and AIDS and sexually transmitted diseases. The detailed content is left up to the school governors to decide with the head teacher. They have, however, made statements about the type of sex education they would like to see taking place. This has focused on a moral framework which should encourage pupils to 'appreciate the value of stable family life, marriage and the responsibilities of parenthood'. They also believe that sex education should not be explicit or go into too much detail.

## Question

What do we mean by 'family'? What different sorts of families exist in this country?

A teenage single mother talking to a class about the difficulties of having children when young

# WHAT PARENTS SAY

Surveys show that most parents fully support their children having sex education at school. A 1994 survey carried out by the Health Education Authority found 94 per cent of parents supported school sex education. Over three quarters of Muslim parents and over 80 per cent of Hindu parents also supported school sex education, despite the fact that many people assume Muslim and Hindu parents are against sex education for their children. A majority of all parents supported sex education beginning in primary schools and only 1 per cent said they would withdraw their children from all sex education lessons.

# THE IMPACT OF SEX EDUCATION

Some people think that if young people are taught about sex it will encourage them to go out and experiment. They believe that sex education increases promiscuity. There is no evidence that sex education does encourage young people to have sex. The World Health Organisation reviewed the findings of 19 international studies which had researched

Some people think sex education encourages young people to have sex. The research evidence shows it does not.

the actual impact of sex education on young people. It concluded that:

- In no study was there evidence of sex education leading to earlier or increased sexual intercourse or activity in the young people who were exposed to it.
- In 6 studies, sex education led either to a delay in the onset of sexual intercourse or to a decrease in sexual activity.
- In 10 studies sex education increased adoption of safer practices amongst those young people who were already having intercourse.

The recent British National Survey of Sexual Attitudes and Lifestyles (see chapter 2) also found that those people who said their main source of sex education was from school were less likely to have started having intercourse when younger than 16 years old, compared to people whose main source of information about sex was from friends, family, books or magazines.

Surveys of teenage girls who become pregnant have shown that one of the reasons they get pregnant is ignorance about how you can become pregnant, contraception and helping services.

The evidence suggests that good school sex education does not lead to increased sexual activity. It can, however, delay the age at which young people begin to have intercourse and lead to safer sexual practices when intercourse occurs.

## THE DILEMMA FOR SCHOOLS

Should schools provide the kind of sex education young people say they want, which tackles a wide range of issues and leaves students to make their own, informed decisions? Or should they limit the scope of sex education and press home 'family values' in line with government thinking? Many teachers feel they will be criticised whatever they do and are unsure about the best way to take sex education forward.

Surveys of what sex education young people want have found that they need accurate and detailed information about a full range of issues. Surveys have also found that they want opportunities to discuss issues openly and honestly without being patronised and told what they should believe or do. They want teachers to be relaxed about the subject and not easily embarrassed or shocked. Rather than avoiding controversial issues young people want to consider them in a way that allows them to reach their own conclusions.

> **66 The young do indeed need protection, not only from physical abuse and emotional cruelty, but also from oversimple beliefs which ignore the complexities of living and loving. Life is a complex business, and everyone needs to be equipped for its challenges and dilemmas. To keep young people in factual ignorance and emotional confusion about intimate aspects of their personal lives is to do them a crippling disservice. 99**

Anthony Grey *Speaking of Sex* Cassel 1993

# ADVICE AND COUNSELLING

The Family Planning Association has suggested that good sex education should:

- Be an integral part of learning, beginning in childhood and continuing into adult life.
- Be for all children, young people and adults, including those with physical, learning or emotional difficulties.
- Encourage exploration of values and moral issues, consideration of sexuality and personal relationships and the development of communication and decision-making skills.
- Foster self-esteem, self-awareness, a sense of moral responsibility and the skills to avoid and resist unwanted sexual experience.

66 Sex education cannot be left to chance or paralysed by power games between adults persecuted by their own inadequacies, uncertainties or over-ripe moral judgements. 99

Doreen Massey, Director of the Family Planning Association 1990

Some students who have a sex related problem turn to teachers for advice and counselling. A sympathetic teacher may be the only adult the young person feels they can turn to. For trust to develop a degree of confidentiality is needed.

In some schools teachers respect confidentiality more than in others. What happens in each school has a lot to do with how the headteacher feels about such issues. In some the head likes to know nearly everything and puts pressure on teachers to pass information on. In others heads encourage staff to keep student confidences unless it is a very serious issue.

The situation has been confused by recent guidance from the government. This suggested that teachers should not give 1 to 1 advice to students under 16 years old without parents knowing and that if they did it could be seen as a criminal offence. It also suggested that if teachers suspected a young person under 16 years of age was having intercourse they should report the young person to the headteacher and their parents. A lot of headteachers and ordinary teachers think this is bad advice and have ignored it but it has put even more pressure on them and made it more difficult to help students when advice is needed.

Some schools have school nurses who can give advice and counselling over sex related issues.

A few schools have teacher/counsellors and some have outsiders (youth workers, social workers etc.) coming in to offer counselling sessions. A few have developed 'peer counselling' where older students are available to support and advise younger

One-to-one tuition can help in all subjects, and allow good relationships to develop between student and teacher. Teachers can also be an important source of support to pupils who have sex-related concerns.

students. There are not many school counsellors in this country, unlike countries like America and the Netherlands where it is more common.

Some schools have developed links with local sexual health services. This has included doctors and nurses being involved in teaching sex education programmes and coming into school to talk about services.

## DEALING WITH SCHOOL GIRL PREGNANCY

Schools need to carefully consider what contribution they can make towards preventing unwanted pregnancy and how they handle situations in which students actually become pregnant. Contraceptive education and encouraging students to use contraceptive services can help with preventing unwanted pregnancy. When girls do become pregnant some schools have offered little support and their main concern has been to get the girl out of the school and hush the issue up for fear that the school will get a bad name or they will be seen to be 'condoning' what the girl has done.

Girls who decide to keep their baby usually leave school and receive little or no education. They may have a few hours of 'home tuition' or go to a special unit for pregnant schoolgirls, if one exists. If the girl does not have the opportunity to continue her studies her future career prospects will be damaged and she may become very isolated. Some schools have encouraged pregnant schoolgirls to stay on at school and tried to

> **A number of girls at my school have become pregnant. Most have had abortions but not all. Those who have gone on with their pregnancy tend to quickly disappear from school. The teachers don't seem to know what to say about it. Some have come back to show off their babies once they are born. They seem so young to be mothers. I don't think they realise how hard it is going to be for them.** *15 year old girl*

ensure they have as normal an education as possible but these schools are in a minority.

## SCHOOL AND HIV/AIDS

Whilst few schools in this country have had cases of students or staff who they know have HIV or AIDS, all schools need to think about what they can best do to support such people if the need arises. One education authority in the North West of England published guidance for its schools on such matters. Ten key principles were identified:

1. There is no evidence of HIV transmission within the education setting.

Schools need to consider how best to deal with HIV and AIDS, even though there have been few known cases in schools.

2. No one should be discriminated against on the grounds that they have HIV or AIDS.

3. Information regarding an individual's HIV status/having AIDS is strictly confidential and is not to be freely discussed between staff, governors or with outside agencies.

4. Children/young people who have HIV or AIDS have a right to full participation in every aspect of education.

5. There is no obligation for anyone to disclose their HIV or AIDS status to anyone else.

6. Support should be available for anyone who has HIV or AIDS, taking account of their own individual needs, circumstances and choice.

7. Discrimination and prejudice against people who have HIV or AIDS should be dealt with immediately and effectively.

8. All education staff should have the opportunity to have access to relevant HIV/ AIDS training.

9. All children and young people should have access to a balanced and thorough ongoing education regarding HIV/ AIDS and related matters.

10. All education establishments should strive to create an atmosphere and environment in which caring, understanding and acceptance prevail.

> 66 **We thought it would be best to keep it quiet. We were worried that other children and their parents would not respond as we hoped, despite the fact that we had done a lot of educational work about HIV.** 99
>
> Teacher of a child who has HIV

**Question**
What do you think would happen in your school if a student was known to have HIV?

# COMBATING SEXUAL HARASSMENT

Sexual harassment is unwanted pestering of a sexual nature and includes physical harassment (such as touching people up), following people, name calling of a sexual nature, whistling etc. It is very common amongst adults and has recently been in the news especially in the form of sexual harassment of women by their bosses at work and women being 'stalked' by men. It also appears to happen a lot amongst young people in and out of school and mainly, but not only, consists of boys harassing girls.

Sexual harassment can be very distressing for the victim but it is often not taken seriously by young people or teachers. Young people themselves have a responsibility to not harass other people and to act to stop other people doing it. Too often people think it is 'just a laugh' and do not realise the misery it can cause. Victims of sexual harassment may become anxious and depressed, may feel they cannot go out or to school and may live in fear. In some cases sexual harassment has been a factor in suicide attempts.

**Question**
Do you, your friends and your school take sexual harassment seriously? What do you think can be done to prevent sexual harassment?

> " These boys kept going on at me about my big breasts. Some of the girls joined in as well. It went on and on. At break. On the corridor. Even in lessons they would send me nasty notes. It got so I didn't want to go to school at all. "
>
> 14 year old girl

Schools can take active steps to do something about it. As well as discussing it in lessons teachers can make sure students know they take it seriously and will act if they find it is happening. Teachers need to be approachable so students who are subjected to sexual harassment know they will be listened to and the issue will be dealt with rather than swept under the carpet.

## COMBATING HOMOPHOBIA

Homophobia is prejudice against gay people. Being young and gay can be particularly difficult. Many young gay people find it difficult to 'come out' to friends or their parents. They may fear being made fun of or being completely rejected. Many young gay people become very isolated and depressed and a number of studies have pointed to them having a higher than average suicide rate.

Often homophobia is based on ignorance, strict religious views or people feeling insecure about their own sexual feelings. Many myths surround homosexuality and a lot of people seem unable to realise that gay people are much the same as everyone else except that they have sexual relationships with people of their own sex. There are gay people in all walks of life. Most of us will know and like gay people who we do not know are gay. Increasingly people are becoming less homophobic and have close friends who are openly gay.

Young people can combat homophobia by making sure they are not prejudiced themselves and by treating gay people the same as they would anyone else. They can also challenge homophobic behaviour by other young people and encourage their schools to take the issue seriously. After all, like sexual harassment and racism, homophobia is really a form of bullying.

## Avert (AIDS Education and Research Trust)
11/13 Denne Parade, Horsham, West Sussex RH12 1JD
01403 210202

## British Pregnancy Advisory Service (BPAS)
Austy Manor, Wootton Wawen, Solihull, West Midlands B95 6BX
01564 793225
Advice and counselling on contraception, abortion, infertility and sexual problems. Local branches all over the country.

## Brook Advisory
165 Grays Inn Road, London WC1X 8UD
0171 713 9000
Advice on contraception, abortion and all aspects of sex.
Information booklets and leaflets. A 24-hour helpline offering advice and information.
0171 617 8000
Clinics for young people in other parts of the country

## Childline
Freepost 1111, London N1 OBR
0800 1111
Confidential freephone helpline for young people.

## Children's Legal Centre
University of Essex, Wivenhoe Park, Colchester, Essex CO4 3SQ
01206 873820
Free legal advice to young people. Information booklets.

## Family Planning Association (FPA)
2-12 Pentonville Road, London N1 9FP
0171 837 5432

## Health Education Authority (HEA)
Hamilton House, Mabledon Place, London WC1H 9TX
0171 383 3833
Leaflets, including some on HIV and STDs.

## Healthwise
First Floor, Cavern Walks, 8 Matthew Street, Liverpool L2 6RE
0151 227 4415
Sex and drugs education teaching resources.

## London Lesbian and Gay Switchboard
Switchboard, London WC1N 3XX
0171 837 7324
24-hour counselling and information for lesbian and gay people.

## National Aids Helpline
PO Box 1577, London NW1 3DW
0800 567123
24-hour freephone helpline.

## Rape Crisis
PO Box 69, London WC1X 9NJ
0171 837 1600
Confidential counselling and advice for rape victims.

## Terrence Higgins Trust
52-54 Grays Inn Road, London WC1X 8JU
0171 831 0330
Helpline 0171 242 1010
Information and advice about HIV and AIDS.

## Local Organisations
There will be local organisations in your area which can provide information and materials on sex-related issues. This should include a Health Promotion Unit (run by the Health Authority) and a Health Education Project (run by the council Education Department).

## IN CANADA
AIDS Committee of Toronto
helpline: 416-340-8844

AIDS Committee of Ottawa
helpline: 613-238-5014

AIDS and Sexual Health Infoline (Ministry of Health, Ontario):
416-392-2437/800-668-2437

AIDS Vancouver Helpline: 604-687-2437
INFO-SIDA, Montreal: 514-521-7432

Project-Dix, Montreal: 514-989-4585 (dealing with questions of sexual orientation)

Action Intervention Jeunesse, Montreal: 514-668-1230

SIDA-Aide, Quebec City: 418-649-0788

Service d'Information en Contraception et Sexualite de Quebec, Quebec City: 418-647-2231

**IN AUSTRALIA**
AIDS COUNCIL OF
VICTORIA PO Box 96
Carlton Sth, VIC 3053
1800133392
TTY 1800 032 665

N.S.W.   150 Albion
Surrey Hills NSW 2010
008 451 6000
TTY 02 332 42 4268

QLD   PO Box 3142
Brisbane QLD 4000
07 3844 1990
TTY 1800 177434

SA   PO Box 907
Kentown SA 5071
1800 888559
TTY 08 362 0306

WA   PO Box 1510
West Perth WA 6872
131025 (state wide)

TAS   PO Box 595F
Hobart 7001
1800 005900

ACT   PO Box 229
Canberra 2601
06 2572855
TTY 06 2472278

NT   PO Box 2826
Darwin NT 0801
1800 011180

FAMILY PLANNING
ASSOCIATION
VICTORIA 270 Church Street
Richmond VIC 3121
03 9429 117

NSW   47 Hercules Street
Chatswood NSW 2067
02 4150 2700

QLD   100 Alfred Street
Fortitude Valley
QLD 4006
07 32525151

SA   17 Philips Street
Kensington SA 5068
08 31 5177

WA   70 Roe Street
Northbridge WA 6003
09 227 6177

TAS   73 Federal Street
North Hobart TAS 7001
002 34 7200

ACT   Childers Street
Canberra ACT 2601
06 247 3077

NT   Rapid Creek Village
Trouwer Road
Rapid Creek NT 0810
08 89480144

# FURTHER READING

The following books are recommended. They should be available from good bookshops or your local library, or try to get them ordered for your school library.

J. Butterworth **Straight talk: how to handle sex** Pan 1993

J. Cousins-Mills **Make it happy, make it safe: What sex is all about** Penguin 1993

The Diagram Group **Sex: a user's manual** New English Library 1988

E. Fenwick and R. Walker **How sex works**, Dorling Kindersley 1994

P. Ferris **Sex and the British – A twentieth century history**, Michael Joseph 1993

J. Goldman **Sex: How? Why? What? – The teenager's guide** Piccadilly Press

J. Hart **So you think you are attracted to the same sex?** Penguin 1984

C. Haste **Rules of desire: sex in Britain** Pimlico 1992

N. Fisher **Your pocket guide to sex** Penguin 1994

A Grey **Speaking of sex** Cassell 1993

E. Marcus **Is it a choice? – Answers to 300 of the most frequently asked questions about gays and lesbians** Harper Collins 1993

J. Mills **Sexwords** Penguin 1993

J. Tavanyar **The Terence Higgins Trust HIV/AIDS book** Thorsons 1992

Kay Wellings et al **Sexual Behaviour in Britain** Penguin 1994

# INDEX